BIBLE STORIES

WITH PRAYERS AND HYMNS

FREDERICK WARNE
Published by the Penguin Group
Penguin Books Ltd, 27 Wrights Lane, London W8 5TZ, England
Penguin Books USA Inc., 375 Hudson Street, New York, N.Y. 10014, USA
Penguin Books Australia Ltd, Ringwood, Victoria, Australia
Penguin Books Canada Ltd, 10 Alcorn Avenue, Toronto, Ontario, Canada M4V 3B2
Penguin Books (N.Z.) Ltd, 182-190 Wairau Road, Auckland 10, New Zealand

Penguin Books Ltd, Registered Offices: Harmondsworth, Middlesex, England

First published 1999 by Frederick Warne

3 5 7 9 10 8 6 4 2

ISBN: 0 7232 4491 X

Printed and bound in Italy by LEGO Spa – Vicenza

BIBLE STORIES

WITH PRAYERS AND HYMNS

Stories written by Dorothy Barker

Illustrated by
CICELY MARY BARKER
WARNE

CONTENTS

Stories

Hymns

Prayers

STORIES

In the Beginning

In the beginning God made the heavens and the earth. He made the sun to shine by day, and the moon and stars by night. He made the great and wide sea, and the fish that live in it. He made the grass, the trees, and every flower that grows upon the earth. He made the tiniest of insects, the animals, small and great, and birds of every colour and size. Into this world, God put man to live, and gave him everything for his happiness.

But then everything began to go wrong. God saw men and women hating one another, and fighting one another. They had forgotten their God, who made them.

Then God decided to find one man who still loved him. This man would be the father of a great family which would have faith in God, and help lead the world back to goodness again.

The Call of Abraham

When Abraham was seventy-five years old, God chose him. "Get up and leave your country, and go into a land which I shall show you, and I will make your name long remembered." Abraham knew at once that it was the voice of the true God, and so he made preparations for his journey. A great company, led by Abraham, started towards the south, and came to the land of Canaan, where they pitched their tents.

God spoke to Abraham again, and said, "This land on which you stand shall belong to your family in the years to come. You shall be the father of a great nation." And God promised Abraham a son, and descendants as numerous as the stars in the sky.

After many years God's promise came true. How happy were Abraham and Sarah when their baby boy was born! Abraham called his son Isaac, and loved him more than anyone else in the world.

Abraham's Sacrifice

Abraham's son, Isaac, grew from a baby to a strong lad, and was the pride and joy of his parents. Then the voice of God spoke to Abraham's heart.

"Take now Isaac, thine only son whom thou lovest, and offer him for a burnt offering up on Mount Moriah."

It was a severe test of Abraham's faith, but without hesitation he made his decision – he would offer his only son as a sacrifice to God.

As they climbed up the steep slope, a thought came to Isaac: "Father," he said, "we have brought the wood and the fire for the burnt offering, but where is the lamb?"

How could the poor old father tell the boy that he was to be the lamb? "My son," he replied, "God will provide a lamb," and Isaac, quite content, walked on in silence.

Abraham piled up big stones for an altar and placed the wood upon it. No one knows in what words he told his son that he was to be a gift to God, but Isaac bravely allowed himself to be laid upon the altar.

The old man was just taking up his knife in a trembling hand when a voice sounded, "Abraham, Abraham! Do not hurt the boy," said the voice, "you have shown how much you love God by offering your only son to Him. Therefore God will bless you, and through you He will bless all the nations upon earth."

And God had also provided a lamb for the sacrifice, for there, close by the altar, was a ram caught by its horns in a thorn bush. Abraham offered the ram to God, then went home with his heart full of love and gratitude, and his only son beside him.

Abraham and Isaac on Mount Moriah

Jacob and Esau

Isaac was getting old, and the time was drawing near when his possessions would be divided between his two sons, Esau and Jacob.

Jacob knew that his father would give the elder son a special blessing, and would pass on to him the promise which God had made to Abraham – but Esau, not Jacob, was the elder son.

Esau was a clever archer. He cared very little for his father's blessing, or for God's promise; he was satisfied if he had a good day's hunting, and a savoury meal when he came in tired and hungry.

How Jacob wished that he were the elder son! If only his were the family blessed by God, so that it might bring a blessing to all the world!

Years went by, until the two brothers were grown men. Their father was so old, and so nearly blind, that he could not distinguish his sons' faces; he knew them apart by their voices. He used to touch them too, and he knew the strong hairy arms and hands of his favourite son Esau.

One day the old man called Esau: "My son," he said, "take your bow and arrows, go out and get me venison. Cook a savoury meal for me such as I love, then I will give you my blessing before I die."

These words were overheard by Isaac's wife, Rebekah, and as soon as she had seen Esau stride away across the fields, she called to her favourite son Jacob and told him what Isaac had said. "Now, my son, obey my voice," she said, "and fetch me two kids from the flock, which I can make into a savoury dish such as your father loves.

Then you shall take it to him, and you will get the elder son's blessing."

Jacob's only fear was that his father would recognize him.

"Esau is a hairy man," he said, "Father will feel the smoothness of my hands."

"Only trust me," replied his mother, "and bring me the kids."

When the meat was ready, Rebekah called Jacob, made him put on a coat belonging to Esau, tied pieces of hairy goat skin on his arms and hands, and sent him thus prepared into his father's tent.

"Come near me, my son," said Isaac, stretching out his hands. "These are Esau's hairy hands," thought the old man, "and the coat is Esau's, it smells of the fields."

So Isaac dined from the meat and wine that Jacob had brought, and then gave him the wished-for blessing.

No sooner had Jacob left the tent than Esau returned from the fields.

"Who art thou?" asked the old man, as he heard Esau's footsteps.

"I am thy first-born son, Esau," replied the young man, "and I have brought you this savoury meat, so that you may eat it and give me your blessing."

Old Isaac began to tremble as he heard these words. "Who is it," he cried, "who has come before you, and brought venison, and taken the blessing?"

Esau wept for the blessing which he began to value when he knew that it could not be his. He left Isaac's tent with anger in his heart, and his mind made up to kill his brother.

When his mother saw him, she guessed his thoughts, and feared for the life of her favourite son, Jacob.

"Obey my voice, Jacob," she entreated, "you must leave

this place, until your brother's anger has passed."

So Jacob, finding that it was the wish of both his parents that he should go, received a last blessing from his father, and left his home without seeing his brother again.

Joseph and his Brothers

Jacob married Leah and Rachel, and had twelve sons. Joseph was Jacob's eleventh and favourite son, and his adventures began when he was quite a small boy.

His father had given him a beautiful many-coloured coat, which was the envy of all his brothers – but it made the brothers jealous and unkind to him.

One night, during the harvest-time, Joseph had a curious dream, that he and his brothers were all binding sheaves of corn in the field, and that the brothers' sheaves bowed down to his sheaf, which stood up in their midst. Another night he dreamed that the sun and moon and eleven stars were all bowing before him.

Joseph, rather unwisely, told these dreams to his father and brothers. "What is this that you have dreamed?" exclaimed Jacob. "Shall I and your brethren bow ourselves to the ground before you?" And the elder brothers hated Joseph because of these dreams.

Soon after this, Joseph's brothers saw him a long way from home tending the flocks. "Let us kill him," they said to one another, "and we will see what will become of his dreams!"

Reuben, the eldest of the brothers, would not agree to this. "Do not take his life," he said, "let us put him down at the bottom of this pit."

When Joseph came near, the brothers seized him roughly, and tore off his coat, then dragged him towards the empty well, let him down to the bottom of it with a rope, and left him there.

While the brothers sat eating their dinner at a little distance from the pit, they noticed a company of merchants

Joseph the Dreamer

travelling slowly, with their heavily laden camels, along the caravan road.

As suddenly and quickly as he had been dropped into the pit, Joseph was drawn out again, and soon found himself a prisoner, marching along the dusty road towards Egypt; while his brothers climbed the hill again, counting their twenty silver pieces, the price of their father's favourite son.

The brothers returned home with their flocks, and went to their father's tent, taking with them the torn remains of Joseph's coloured coat. "It is my son's coat," cried Jacob in great distress, "an evil beast has devoured him. I shall mourn for Joseph as long as I live!"

Jacob wept for many days at the loss of his favourite boy, and his elder sons kept their secret, never thinking that God could bring good out of their evil deed, and that Joseph's dreams might yet come true.

Joseph in Egypt

Joseph found himself a slave in a big Egyptian house, the home of Potiphar, an officer in the body-guard of Pharaoh, King of Egypt.

He was a good slave, and in time he was made head of all the servants, and overseer of the household. But his master's wife disliked him, and made up wicked and untrue stories about him, until her husband decided he must send Joseph to prison.

But he kept his faith in God, and was so courageous and cheerful that he won the prison keeper's trust and befriended the other prisoners. The chief butler and chief baker from the king's palace were among them. One night both men had strange dreams. "Tell me your dreams," said Joseph kindly, "for my God can show me the meaning of them."

Joseph listened while they told him of three clusters of ripe grapes and three baskets of sweet cakes which they had seen. The butler dreamed that he had squeezed the juice of the ripe grapes into Pharaoh's cup; the baker dreamed that, when he reached the king, his baskets, which he carried on his head, were empty, because the birds had eaten the cakes.

"This is the meaning of the dreams," said Joseph. "The three bunches of grapes and the three baskets are three days. In three days' time the butler will be handing Pharaoh his cup of wine at a feast; but the baker will bake for the king no more."

The dreams came true as Joseph had said, and the butler was sent for to return to the palace. "Remember me when you are in the king's presence," entreated Joseph. But the butler forgot all about Joseph, until the king had a strange dream, two years later.

The king had seen in his dream seven fat cows coming up from the River Nile, and feeding upon the grass on the banks. Then up came seven very thin hungry-looking cows, and though they devoured the seven fat ones, they looked no better for the meal.

The wise men sought in vain to explain this curious dream. Then the butler remembered Joseph, and he was hurried to the palace, to interpret the dream.

"God has sent this dream to show Pharaoh what will come to pass in the land of Egypt," began Joseph. "The seven fat cows are seven years of plenty. The seven thin cows are seven years of famine. Let Pharaoh choose a wise man who will build barns and store up the corn which grows during the years of plenty, that he may be able to sell it to the people, and they will have bread to eat in the years of famine."

The king knew Joseph was this wise man. He drew his ring from his finger, and gave it to Joseph. "Thou shalt be overseer of my house, and governor of all the land of Egypt!"

After seven years of plenty came the time, foretold by Joseph, when the earth was parched and no corn would grow. So the hungry Egyptians flocked to Joseph, and he ordered that his grain storehouses should be opened, and the overseers sold corn to the people. The news spread that there was plenty of corn in Egypt, and Joseph soon had men from many lands coming to buy from his well-filled barns.

~

Ten men bowed their faces to the earth before Joseph, the governor of Egypt. They spoke in Hebrew, asking to buy corn to fill the empty sacks which they had brought with them from the land of Canaan.

Joseph knew his brothers at once – but he would not make himself known to them yet. He sent them home, demanding that they return with their youngest brother, Benjamin. He then gave orders that the sacks which the men had brought should be filled with corn, and that, unknown to them, their money should be returned to them on top of their sacks; and that Simeon should be bound and kept a prisoner as a guarantee of their return.

The brothers returned home to tell their father of the rough way in which the governer had treated them, and of the finding of the money in the top of their sacks. "Joseph is gone, and Simeon is gone, and now you would take Benjamin away from me!" cried the old man. Unwillingly, he let his youngest son go, and sent presents as a peace offering for the cruel governor.

Again the brothers stood before Joseph, and Benjamin was with them. They bowed low and presented their gifts. "Is your father well, the old man of whom you spoke?" asked Joseph, "and this must be your youngest brother – God be gracious to thee, my son." He invited the brothers to dine with him, at his own table, and Benjamin was given five times as much as any of the others.

Early next morning the brothers started on their homeward journey, with their sacks filled according to Joseph's instructions. They had not gone far, when they were stopped by Joseph's steward, who was running after them. "Why have you done this?" he cried. "You have taken the silver cup from which my lord drinks!"

"God forbid that we should do such a thing!" exclaimed the brothers. But to their horror and surprise the silver cup was found in Benjamin's sack! They could not leave Benjamin, so they all turned around and accompanied the steward back to Joseph's house.

"What is it you have done?" said Joseph gravely.

"The man in whose sack my cup was found shall be my bondman – the rest of you can go in peace."

In great distress Judah went forward and stood before Joseph. "We cannot go home without our youngest brother, for our father loves the boy! We had another brother, but he is dead, and if we lose Benjamin my father will die of sorrow. I pray you, my lord, let me be your bondman in his place."

Joseph was touched by this appeal. He could not keep his secret any longer; he must end their distress.

"I am Joseph," he said. "God has been with me here; it was God, and not you, who sent me here, to save many lives during famine. Come near me my brothers!" and Joseph kissed his brothers and wept over them.

And Joseph said, "Bring my father and all our family into Egypt and we will make the land of Goshen our home."

When the brothers returned to their father with the wonderful news, he could not believe it. Then at night God spoke to the old man in a dream, and said, "I am the God of thy father; fear not to go down into Egypt, for I will there make of thee a great nation;" and Jacob's last doubt was taken away.

The great company travelled slowly from Canaan, along the caravan road to Egypt. Joseph drove his chariot to meet his father. They wept for joy, and Jacob said, "Now I can die in peace, for I have seen thy face again!"

The Baby in the Bulrushes

Time passed, and Jacob's descendants, the Israelites, became known to the Egyptians as "the children of Israel."

There was great and terrible trouble in the land of Goshen. The families of the Israelites had grown so large, that they were called tribes, and the new king was afraid that some day they might join with his enemies and fight against him. So he made the men work for him.

They had to labour all the long hot days making bricks and building great cities for him.

But still the Pharoah felt the Israelites were a threat to him. So he ordered that every new-born baby, if it were a boy, should be thrown into the River Nile. There was a man and his wife, belonging to the tribe of Levi, who had three children, Miriam, and Aaron, and a baby boy.
When the baby was born, his mother could not bear to part with him. She disobeyed the king's cruel command, and hid her baby.

But when the child was three months old, she felt she could not hide him any longer; he was getting bigger and stronger, and might be discovered any day.

Then the poor mother thought of one last plan to try and save her baby's life. She would place him on the river bank just where the king's daughter came down to bathe; perhaps the princess would see him and have pity on him.

Early the next morning she laid her baby in a little cradle of plaited papyrus reeds, put it down among the bulrushes on the bank of the Nile, and with many tears and prayers to God, she left him.

Presently the baby awoke. Strange hands were lifting him from his cradle, strange voices were speaking to him,

Finding Moses

and he began to cry.

His sister Miriam crept out from the tall rushes, where she had been hiding. She saw the princess herself looking very kindly at the crying baby, and heard her say to her ladies: "This must be one of the Hebrews' children. Poor little thing, I should like to have him for my own."

Miriam stepped eagerly up to the princess:

"Shall I fetch a Hebrew woman to take care of the baby, and nurse it for you?" she asked. The princess liked this suggestion. Miriam went to fetch her mother.

With joy and thankfulness the poor mother took her baby home again. The princess named the baby Moses, and when he was about three years old she sent for him to live with her at the palace; and treated him just as though he were her own son.

Moses found out that he really belonged to the children of Israel, and one day he went away by himself to the land of Goshen, to see his brethren.

The sights that he saw distressed him very much. There were the poor Hebrew men toiling in the brick fields, with stern Egyptian task-masters standing by them with whips, and beating them if they did not work fast enough.

Moses watched this cruel treatment until he could bear it no longer, then he lost his temper. He rushed at one of the task-masters, and beat him to death.

When Pharaoh heard of this, he was very angry. He would not have anyone interfering with his work in the brick fields – Moses must be killed!

But Moses fled from Egypt, and went to live in the land of Midian.

For forty years Moses lived as a shepherd in Midian.

Then, one day, when Moses was out with the flocks, he

noticed a bush at a little distance from him, which seemed to be burning. An angel stood in the midst of the flames.

Moses covered his face with his hands – he knew now that he was in the presence of the great God of Israel.

"I have seen the sorrows of my people, and I have heard their cry," said the voice of God. "I will send thee to bring forth my people out of Egypt."

Moses was afraid when he heard this – the task seemed far too great for him.

"I will be with thee," said the voice, "I will teach thee what thou shalt speak. Behold, thy brother Aaron cometh to meet thee. I will be with thy mouth and with his mouth; he shall be thy spokesman to the people."

The flames died down, leaving the bush fresh and green, and quite unhurt by the fire.

Together the brothers left Midian, to return to Goshen with the good news that the mighty God of Israel was going to deliver his people from their bondage. Moses was to set his people free, and lead them out of Egypt.

Gideon

Gideon was in the wine-press, well hidden by the high walls, beating the husks from his father's little store of wheat. The threshing must be done very secretly for fear of the Midianites, a tribe of desert raiders.

The years had passed. Moses had led his people safely out of Egypt and into the Promised Land. But now the people had forgotten Moses, and the ten laws of God which he carried down from Mount Sinai. They forgot their promise to serve only one God, and began to worship the gods of the nations around them, which were not gods, but only figures of wood or stone.

Even Gideon's father, Joash, had an altar to Baal in his garden. Then trouble came. The Midianites began robbing and destroying the land.

At last, in great humility, the people cried to God to deliver them. Would he hear them, and answer their prayer?

A stranger was standing quietly beside Gideon in the wine-press.

"The Lord has sent thee to save Israel from the hand of Midian," said the angel messenger.

During the next few days, Gideon assembled his army. They came in great numbers, thirty-two thousand of them; but the Midianite army, encamped in the valley, was greater.

At night God spoke to Gideon, and said: "The men that are with thee are too many; if I give them the victory, they will boast that their own strength has saved them from the enemy."

The following day Gideon proclaimed, "Whoever is afraid, let him return to his home," and twenty-two thousand men left the camp.

Gideon and the angel messenger

That night God told Gideon that his army was still too large.

Gideon then took his ten thousand men to a stream of water, to let them drink before the battle. Most of them threw themselves down on the ground, put their mouths to the water, and drank greedily. The rest took up a little water in the palms of their hands to drink.

"By the three hundred men who lapped water from their hands will we save Israel," cried Gideon; "the others can return to their tents."

That night, when darkness fell and the enemy slept, Gideon placed his three hundred men around the Midianite camp. Each man had a trumpet in one hand, and a torch concealed in a pitcher in the other.

A little before midnight Gideon blew a blast on his trumpet, threw down his pitcher, held on high his flaming torch, and cried aloud, "The sword of the Lord, and of Gideon!"

Immediately the three hundred men blew on their trumpets, the three hundred pitchers crashed to the ground, three hundred lighted torches flared around the camp, and three hundred voices shouted the battle-cry, "The sword of the Lord, and of Gideon!"

To the Midianites, suddenly aroused, the noise appeared to come from a vast army, all round their camp, and they were terrified.

They ran out of their tents, falling over one another and fighting each other in the darkness. They fled away to the mountains, pursued by the triumphant Israelites. They crossed the Jordan to their own land, and returned no more to trouble Israel.

The Child Samuel

It was a feast-day in Shiloh, and the Israelites were assembled there to worship God.

Among the crowd were Hannah and her husband. Hannah was not joining in the feasting and rejoicing, she was too unhappy. For years it had been her greatest wish to have a child, but she was barren.

She went into the dimly lighted tent and, weeping bitterly, she began to pray: "O Lord of Hosts, if thou wilt give me a child, then I will give him unto the Lord all the days of his life."

In time God answered Hannah's prayer. How great was her joy when her baby son, Samuel, was born! But in all her pleasure Hannah did not forget her promise to give her boy to God; so when he was four years old she sought out Eli, the old priest in the tabernacle. "For this child I prayed," she said, "and the Lord has granted my petition. Therefore I have lent him to the Lord as long as he lives."

Hannah left her little boy with Eli; he would now learn to serve the great God of Israel.

Samuel kept everything clean and bright in the tabernacle. Each year, at the time of the feast, his mother came to see him, and to bring him a new coat which she had made.

Samuel grew fond of Eli, and soon discovered that he was greatly troubled by the bad conduct of his two sons. They were priests, but their wicked lives made them unfit for their holy work. One night, when his work was done, Samuel lay down to sleep in his small curtained room close to the tabernacle. Suddenly he heard a voice calling, "Samuel, Samuel!"

Samuel heard the voice again

He sprang up quickly and opened the curtains which separated his little room from Eli's. "Here am I," he said, "for you called me."

"I called not," replied the old man; "lie down again."

No sooner was Samuel lying in his place, than he heard the voice again. Surely it was Eli calling this time. He went to the priest's bedside. "Here am I, for you did call me," he said.

"I called not, my son," said Eli; "lie down again."

Samuel did not know that it was the voice of God that he had heard, and when he was called yet a third time, he rose up as before and went to Eli. "Here am I, for you did call me," he said.

"It must be that the Lord is speaking to the child," thought Eli to himself. "Go and lie down," he said to Samuel, "and if you are called again, you shall say, Speak, Lord, for Thy servant heareth."

Samuel, full of wonder, lay down on his blanket, and listened. Soon, in the darkness, he heard the voice again, "Samuel, Samuel!"

"Speak, Lord, for Thy servant heareth," answered the boy. Samuel then heard these solemn words: "I have said that the family of Eli shall be priests for ever, but now, because of their wickedness, his sons shall both die; and I will raise up another family of faithful priests in Israel."

In the morning Samuel went to Eli, and gave the old man this terrible message. "It is the Lord's will," said Eli sadly.

Some years later the Philistines made ready for battle against Israel. The sons of Eli took the golden Ark of God from its place in the tabernacle, and carried it into the camp, thinking its presence there might give Israel the victory.

When a messenger came running from the camp saying,

"The sons of Eli are dead and the Ark of God is taken!" the shock was too great for Eli, and he died the same day.

The people then turned to Samuel for guidance, for all believed that God had chosen him to be a prophet in Israel.

In time, God would ask Samuel to anoint the chosen king of Israel.

David, the Shepherd Boy

David loved his quiet shepherd's life, with the lambs bleating, and the sheep grazing peacefully around him.

David's thoughts were of the God who had made this lovely world. Samuel the prophet had sent for him and anointed his head with oil – as a sign that God had chosen David to be the future king of Israel. David had returned to the hills near Bethlehem to mind his father's sheep, but God seemed nearer to him now, watching over him like a loving father.

The Ark of God had been returned to the Israelites, but they were still at war with their old enemies, the Philistines.

One day a servant came in haste to fetch David from the hills; he must bring his harp and come at once to King Saul, for the king was ill and very unhappy, and thought that music might soothe his troubled spirit.

David took his harp and began to play; in time the sweetness of the music comforted the king's sad heart, so that he was able to rise up and return to his army.

The Israelites were encamped on the side of a hill, the Philistines were on an opposite hill; a small stream flowed along the valley between them, and both armies were ready for battle.

Each day the Philistines sent out their champion, Goliath of Gath, fully armed, with a shield-bearer before him, to stand on the hillside and shout across the valley: "Choose you a man, and if he be able to fight with me and kill me, then we will be your servants; but if I kill him, then shall you serve us!"

The armies of Israel trembled when they heard these words, and no man was brave enough to fight alone with the giant Philistine.

One morning David came into the camp to see his brothers. He heard Goliath's voice thundering across the valley, and he was amazed to learn that the Israelites were all afraid. "I will go and fight with this Philistine," he said at once.

David was taken straight to the king's tent; but when King Saul saw the shepherd lad, he said gently: "You are not able to fight, for you are but a youth, and the Philistine is a man of war."

"The Lord who saved me from the paw of the lion and the paw of the bear when I kept my father's sheep, will deliver me," said David.

"Go, then," said the king, "and the Lord shall be with you."

Unarmed, except for his staff, his shepherd's sling, and five smooth stones which he picked up from the stream, the boy went boldly forward to meet the giant.

David, the Shepherd Boy

The months went by, and still no rain came to water the thirsty earth. People were starving for want of bread and water, but the widow of Sarepta and her little son had just enough meal in their barrel, and oil in their jar for each day's need; and the prophet Elijah stayed with them and shared their humble food.

One day when Elijah entered the house, the poor woman sat weeping and clasping her boy in her arms. He had been taken ill that day and he was dead.

"Why did you ever come here, O man of God!" she cried as soon as she saw the prophet; "did you come to punish me for my past sins by killing my son?"

Elijah was sorry for the mother's grief. "Give me thy son," he said gently. She allowed him to take the child from her, and he carried him up to his own small room, and laid him on the bed.

The prophet prayed very earnestly to God and said, "O Lord my God, I pray thee, let this child's soul come into him again."

At these words the little boy awoke, as from a sleep; his spirit had returned.

Elijah lifted him from the bed and carried him to his poor unhappy mother. "See," he said, "thy son liveth!"

"Now I know that thou art indeed a man of God," cried the widow, as she held her living son tightly in her arms; "and the word of the Lord in thy mouth is truth!"

Three long years went by, with no shower of rain nor drop of dew to refresh the thirsty land of Israel, before a strong west wind began to blow. Clouds came quickly up from the sea till all the sky was black, and a welcome heavy rain began to fall.

Elijah and the widow's son

The Prophet of the Most High

Zacharias, the old priest, entered alone into the Holy Place of the Temple, to burn incense on the golden altar. His own disappointment at having no son was forgotten as the aged man performed his priestly work. His heart was full of hope that the coming of the Messiah foretold by the prophets was drawing near.

Suddenly the priest was troubled to see that he was not alone in the Holy Place – an angel of God was standing at the right side of the altar. "Fear not," said the angel. "Your prayers have been heard. You and your wife Elisabeth shall have a son, and you shall call him John. He shall go before the children of Israel as Elijah the prophet, to make ready a people prepared for the Lord."

"How shall this be?" Zacharias asked the angel, "For my wife and I are now old people."

"I am Gabriel, and I am sent to bring this good news," replied the angel. "You shall be dumb and not able to speak until these things come to pass, because you have not believed my words."

Zacharias returned over the hills to his wife Elisabeth; his thoughts full of what had happened.

In the village of Nazareth, among the hills of Galilee, lived Elisabeth's young cousin Mary. She was gentle and good, and spent much time in prayer for the coming of the Messiah.

One day when she was quiet and alone, the angel Gabriel appeared to her. Mary was troubled at the sight of this splendid messenger, but his words reassured her. "Fear not, Mary," he said, "for thou hast found favour with God. Thou shalt have a son, and thou shalt call him Jesus. He shall be great, and shall be called the Son of the Most High. And Elisabeth thy kinswoman shall have a son in her old age – for with God all things are possible."

Soon the glad news spread among Elisabeth's neighbours that she had a baby boy. "He shall be called John," she said.

"But there is none of thy kindred called by this name," argued the neighbours; so Zacharias was appealed to.

The old man was still unable to speak, so he took his waxen writing tablet, and to the surprise of the company he wrote, "His name is John."

At that moment the power of speech came back to him, and he thanked God for his infant son.

Zacharias and Elisabeth watched their son grow into a quiet and thoughtful lad. John learnt all that Zacharias could tell him of the coming Messiah, and he knew that he, himself, had a message from God for the people. He must tell them that the King was at hand – they must be ready, to receive him.

The Birth of Jesus

Down the Roman road towards Jerusalem walked Joseph, the carpenter, leading a donkey on which rode Mary, his wife.

The three days' journey was nearly over; before night they would reach Bethlehem.

Joseph went straight to the inn when they arrived at Bethlehem; he was anxious to find a comfortable resting place for Mary, his young wife, who was awaiting the birth of her promised Son.

They found the inn courtyard crowded with camels and donkeys, all tied up in the centre, and every little room occupied by noisy travellers settling themselves in their blankets for the night.

"No room," said the landlord; but at Joseph's urgent entreaty, he showed them a stable, saying that they might spend the night there.

By the light of a lantern Joseph tied up his donkey, and made as soft a bed as he could for Mary, with their striped blankets spread upon the straw. But they had little sleep that night, for soon after midnight, while all Bethlehem lay silent under the starlit sky, Mary's infant Son was born.

In the humble stable was a wooden manger filled with hay for the beasts to eat. This would make a soft, sweet-scented bed, and there Mary gently laid her new-born Baby.

The angels knew that this was the Son of God, and the sky grew bright with the glory of heaven as they came to proclaim the birth of Jesus. But only a few poor shepherds keeping watch by their sheep on the hills of Bethlehem saw their splendour. As they lay round their fire, wrapped in their heavy coats, with the pale forms of their flock lying near

The new-born Baby sleeps

them, they were startled to see a shining angel.

"Fear not," said the angel, "I bring you good tidings of great joy. For there is born to you today, a Saviour, who is Christ the Lord. You shall find the Babe, wrapped in swaddling clothes, and lying in a manger."

The light of heaven shone round the shepherds, and the sky was filled with angels singing. The angels flew back to heaven, the glory faded, and the shepherds left their sheep on the hillside, and went into the sleeping city in the early dawn.

They found the little stable; and creeping quietly to the doorway, they peeped in. By the dim lantern light they could see a cow and the donkey standing there, they could see Joseph anxiously watching over the young mother, and in the midst was the sight they had come to see — the new-born Baby, sleeping on his bed of hay.

Silently they looked; then they went away praising God, to tell of all that they had heard and seen on this first Christmas morning.

Wise Men from the East

Unnoticed by the people passing up and down the streets of Jerusalem, Joseph and Mary made their way to the Temple, and entered one of the big gates. Joseph carried a small cage containing two pigeons, and his wife held her six weeks' old Baby in her arms.

They had come to present the infant Jesus to God in the temple, and to offer their gift of two young pigeons, as the law of Moses commanded.

An old man approached them as they walked across the wide court – a good old man, often to be seen in the Temple, watching and praying for the coming of the Messiah.

Joseph and Mary did not know old Simeon, but they stopped and let him take the Baby into his arms. As he looked at the infant face, he knew that the great wish of his life had come true; here at last was the promised King, and looking up to heaven, he said, "Lord, now lettest thou thy servant depart in peace, according to thy word, for mine eyes have seen thy salvation."

Some months later all Jerusalem was troubled by the arrival of three splendidly dressed strangers on camels, attended by servants, and asking: "Where is he that is born King of the Jews, for we have seen his star in the East, and are come to worship him."

Herod the Great, king of Judea, was angry and afraid when he heard of the arrival of these strangers from the East. Who was this King they were seeking?

The three Wise Men from the East were brought into Herod's presence, and questioned closely about the star which they had seen. They were learned old men, who had spent

Simeon and the Baby Jesus

The Voice in the Wilderness

Jesus settled down to a quiet village life, growing from childhood to manhood, beloved by all who knew him.

One day, a young man stood on the banks of the river Jordan surrounded by a crowd of men and women. His limbs were tanned by sun and wind, and his face full of earnest purpose, for he had a message to all who would listen.

This was John, the son of Zacharias and Elisabeth.

From the towns and villages of Judea, and from Galilee, came rich and poor, fishermen, tax collectors, Roman soldiers, and even Pharisees from Jerusalem to hear this new preacher.

"I am the voice of one crying in the wilderness. Make ye ready the way of the Lord," said John.

One by one those who were sorry for their past sins went up to John, confessing that they were not fit to meet the Messiah. One by one John took them down to the river and dipped them in it, as a sign that their sins were washed away.

"I baptize you with water," said John, "but there is one coming after me who is mightier than I, and he will baptize you with the Holy Spirit."

Among the crowd round the Baptist was Jesus, the carpenter of Nazareth.

Even Jesus wished to be baptized. It is true that the Son of God had no sin to confess – but his baptism would mark a change in his life; he had laid aside his carpenter's tools, for he had other work to do.

After the baptism, as Jesus stepped out of the water, a sudden beam of light shone from the sky, and the Holy Spirit, in the form of a dove, came down and rested upon him.

On the banks of the river Jordan

At the same time he heard a voice saying: "This is my beloved Son, in whom I am well pleased."

The long years of waiting were over, the Messiah had come.

That same day Jesus went away among the lonely hills and rocks of the wilderness, and there spent long days and nights, heedless of burning sun, or hunger, or howling wolves, lost in deep thought and prayer.

How should he tell his people that God loved them still, and show them the way to the Kingdom of Heaven? Should he with his divine power turn the stones of the wilderness into bread to feed the poor? Should he proclaim himself the King of all the nations? No one knows how hard it was for Jesus to put aside these tempting ideas.

At last he made his decision to live among men, to teach, and heal, and love; to show them how to live, and, if need be, how to die, and so turn the kingdoms of this world into the Kingdom of Heaven.

After forty days Jesus appeared again among the crowds round the Baptist.

"Behold the Lamb of God," said John, and a little group of fishermen from the lake of Galilee watched him, and followed him at a short distance, longing to speak to him.

They soon had their chance, for Jesus turned and saw them. They made friends at once; and the next day when Jesus started off to return to Galilee, he was accompanied by four fishermen, Peter and his brother Andrew, James and his brother John; all eager to follow their new Master.

The Hungry Multitude

Jesus performed many wonderful miracles as he went about among the towns and villages of Galilee, teaching the people and healing the sick. A great number of men and women followed him, and they called themselves his disciples, because they were learning from him.

One day Jesus chose twelve men out of this throng of disciples, and explained to them that they must now begin the new work for which he had called them. They were to go out into the villages, to proclaim the coming of the Kingdom of Heaven, and to heal the sick, as they had seen Jesus himself do. They should be called apostles, which is a name for those who are sent out.

Among the twelve were the four fishermen, Matthew the tax-gatherer, Philip, Nathaniel, Thomas, and Judas Iscariot.

Away they went, two and two, each with a staff in his hand, but taking neither bread nor money for his journey; they were to depend on the kindness of the village people for their food and lodging.

At an appointed time the apostles met again at Capernaum, eager to tell Jesus all that they had said and done.

"Come apart with me, into a quiet place, and rest a while," said Jesus; so they launched a boat, and sailed across to the other side of the lake of Galilee.

They landed at a place where the grassy hill sloped to the shore, they climbed to the top, and threw themselves down among the wild flowers. They could see the winding sandy road which led from village to village round the lake.

And they saw men, women, and children, some walking, some running, hundreds of them, perhaps thousands, crowding along that sandy road.

Jesus feeds the Hungry Multitude

Jesus showed no disappointment that the crowds had spoilt his peaceful day. He welcomed them kindly, and spent the whole day talking to them, and curing any who were sick.

Towards evening the people became hungry.

Andrew came up then. "Master," he said, "there is a boy here who has five barley loaves and two small fishes – but what are they among so many?"

The boy came forward and offered his little loaves and fishes; but surely even Jesus could not make them enough to feed five thousand men, besides women and children!

Jesus took them in his hands; he gave thanks to God for them, then divided them among the twelve apostles; and they handed portions of bread and fish to all the hungry people who sat round on the grass, until everyone was satisfied.

When the meal was over, there were still pieces of food left upon the grass. "Gather up the fragments that remain, that nothing be wasted," said Jesus; and the people looked on in surprise while the apostles filled twelve baskets with broken pieces which were left over from the five barley loaves and the two small fishes.

When Jesus returned to Capernaum, he found the crowds there were even greater than before; they had come from the towns and villages round the lake, seeking him.

"You seek me because you ate of the loaves and were filled," he told them; "you should rather seek the bread of God, which comes down from heaven."

"Lord, evermore give us this bread!" they cried. "I am the Bread of Life," replied Jesus; "he that comes to me shall never hunger, and he that believes in me shall never thirst."

The Last Supper

Jesus knew that the priests and Pharisees were growing more and more jealous of him; he knew that they would presently wish to take his life; and he tried to warn his apostles that danger awaited him when they went up to Jerusalem for the Feast of the Passover. But the apostles did not believe that any harm would come to their beloved Master.

"Master, where shall we eat the Passover?" inquired Peter and John on Thursday morning.

"Go into the city," answered Jesus, "and when you see a man carrying a pitcher of water, follow him home; ask for the head of the house. He will show you a large upper room, furnished; there make ready."

In the evening, Jesus and the twelve apostles met in the upper room, and found all ready for them – the usual Passover supper of lamb roasted with bitter herbs, flat loaves of unleavened bread, and wine to drink.

No one but Jesus seemed to notice that Judas Iscariot sat silent and furtive, as though he had something to hide – he had indeed a terrible secret, for in his pocket were thirty silver coins, given him by the priests in return for his promise to lead them privately to Jesus.

There was a pitcher of water standing by the door of the upper room, also a bowl and a towel. When all the apostles were seated, Jesus got up quietly, took the towel and bowl of water, and himself washed his disciples' feet. In shame they watched him doing the humble work which they had all been too proud to do. When he had finished, Jesus said, "If I then, your Lord and Master, have washed your feet, ye ought also to wash one another's feet."

During the supper the twelve could see that Jesus was troubled, and presently he said, "Truly I say to you that one of you shall betray me to my enemies."

Then he turned to Judas Iscariot, and said, "What thou doest, do quickly," and Judas, seeing that Jesus knew his secret, got up and hurried from the room, out into the night.

The meal went on, and presently Jesus stood up and took a loaf of bread into his hands. He gave thanks for it, then broke it, and put a piece into the hand of each apostle.

"Take and eat this," he said; "for this is my body which is broken for you – do this in remembrance of me."

Then Jesus took a cup of wine, and handed it to each in turn. "Drink ye all of this," he said; "for this is my blood which is shed for you and for many – do this in remembrance of me."

The apostles began to feel afraid and very unhappy. They did not know that the days would come when they would meet together with joy to share the holy bread and wine in memory of their Master.

Jesus knew how his disciples felt, so he tried to cheer them. "This is my commandment, that ye love one another, even as I have loved you. Greater love hath no man than this, that a man lay down his life for his friends. Ye are my friends, if ye do the things which I command you."

When Jesus had finished speaking, and the Last Supper was over, they all stood up and sang an evening hymn, then went out together into the quiet streets.

Good Friday

Pontius Pilate, the Roman governor in Jerusalem, was called up early on Friday morning by a clamouring crowd, who had brought a prisoner for his judgment. Pilate was surprised to see so calm and dignified a prisoner.

The excited priests on the palace steps began to accuse Jesus. "He stirs up the people by preaching throughout all Judea," cried one. "He says that he is the Messiah, a king," added another. "He calls himself the Son of God," said a third.

Pontius Pilate turned to Jesus. "Behold how many things they witness against you. Do you answer nothing?" he said.

Jesus had heard the witnesses mix truth with untruth, and he preferred to keep silence before them; so Pilate took him into the judgment hall and asked him privately, "Are you the King of the Jews?"

"My kingdom is not of this world; if my kingdom were of this world, then would my servants fight for me," replied Jesus.

"Are you a king then?" persisted Pilate.

"I am a king; and all who know the truth, know that my words are true," said Jesus.

Truth? Pilate did not know the truth, but he could see that this quiet, kingly man was no ordinary prisoner; he could not sentence this man to death.

Silence fell on the crowd when Pontius Pilate again appeared at the palace door.

"I find no fault in the man," he announced, "and it is the custom that I release one prisoner at the time of the Passover; shall I release unto you the King of the Jews?"

No, this would not please the jealous priests. "Not this man, but the thief, Barabbas!" they cried, and the crowd took up the cry, "Not this man, but Barabbas!"

Pilate was unwilling to condemn an innocent man to death, and he turned back into the palace. There the soldiers had put a purple robe upon Jesus, and a crown of plaited thorns on his head, and were calling out with cruel, mocking laughter, "Hail, King of the Jews!"

Pilate ordered them to lead Jesus out on to the palace steps, and he called to the crowd, "Behold your king." He hoped that the sight of Jesus, standing silent and unafraid before them, would melt their hard hearts. But no, the people, urged by the priests, cried out again and again, "Let him be crucified!"

Knowing that he did a cowardly thing, Pilate delivered up Jesus to be crucified.

On a hill called Calvary, outside the wall of Jerusalem, stood three dark crosses.

On two of them hung thieves, suffering punishment for their wickedness.

On the centre cross Jesus was fastened by great nails through his hands and feet. He who had done no wrong was suffering for the jealousy, hatred, and cowardice of wicked men.

Close to the cross stood Mary, his mother, and John, his beloved disciple, trying to comfort one another, as they waited by him with breaking hearts.

Standing around in little groups were the chief priests and some of the Jews. "If thou art the Son of God, come down from the cross!" they said; then turned away, scornfully shaking their heads and saying: "He saved others, himself he cannot save."

Presently heavy clouds came up and hid the sun; the earth trembled, and darkness veiled the hill of Calvary, so that the crowds who watched from afar returned to Jerusalem in great fear.

For three long hours the darkness lasted; and no one

knows what Jesus suffered then. All the evil of the world had closed around him, and he felt the bitterness of separation from God. But the powers of evil, strong though they were, could not kill the brave Spirit of the Son of God.

At last, those watching by him in the darkness heard his joyful cry. "It is finished! Father, into thy hands I commend my spirit!" He bowed his head, and his Spirit, freed from his body, went to join the waiting spirits in happy paradise.

Towards sunset a very sad little procession walked slowly down the hill of Calvary, to a garden in which was a rocky cave. Joseph of Arimathea and Nicodemas were carrying Jesus' body, carefully wrapped in fine white linen, and they laid it gently in the cave. Mary, Jesus' mother, with Mary Magdalen and some other faithful women from Galilee, followed into the garden, and took a last look at Jesus' body, lying so still and peaceful, before a heavy stone was rolled in front of the entrance to the rocky tomb.

With hearts full of sorrow the little party left the garden, to spend the next day, which was the Jews' Sabbath, preparing sweet spices to bring to the tomb on Sunday morning.

The chief priests then went to Pontius Pilate. "The tomb must be watched," they said, "lest his disciples steal him away, and say that he is risen from the dead."

Pilate allowed them to have a guard of soldiers, and they went away well satisfied that their wicked work was complete.

In the upper room in Jerusalem, Jesus' apostles were gathered, frightened and despairing. All the joy was gone out of their lives. Their Master, whom they loved, was dead, and buried in Joseph's tomb. Never were men more disappointed and miserable. This was the end of all their bright hopes.

But was it really the end?

Easter Day

Early on Sunday morning Mary Magdalen and the other women made their way through the quiet streets to Joseph's garden.

They remembered that a great stone had been rolled in front of the tomb, and that the Jews had sent soldiers to guard it day and night. When they reached the garden they were surprised to see no soldiers there, and then to their horror they found that the stone was already rolled aside, and someone had taken Jesus' body away. They hastened to the upper room where the unhappy apostles were gathered.

"They have taken away our Lord from the garden," cried the women, "and we know not where they have laid him!"

Peter and John sprang up at once. Along the street and into the garden ran the two men, hardly knowing what they expected to find. John reached the tomb first, and peered into the darkness. He could see the white linen gleaming there. Peter came up, and went boldly into the cave, followed by John. Together they gazed at the linen wrappings which lay flat and empty – Jesus' body was not there!

Filled with amazement, but scarcely understanding yet what had happened, the two men went back to their friends.

Mary Magdalen had followed them into the garden and was weeping bitterly there. She had wanted to do the last service she could for her Lord and Master, by putting sweet spices in his tomb; and now someone had taken his body away.

Presently, she turned to the door of the cave and looked in. To her surprise she saw two angels sitting there, one at the head and one at the feet, where Jesus' body had lain.

"Woman, why weepest thou?" they asked.

"Mary!" said the voice

"Because they have taken away my Lord, and I know not where they have laid him," she cried in great distress.

Then another voice behind her spoke. "Woman, why weepest thou? Whom seekest thou?"

She turned quickly, and saw through her tears someone standing there.

"Mary!" said the voice – that wonderful voice which she never thought to hear again – Jesus' voice.

Some of the apostles were still in the upper room when Mary Magdalen came into the midst of them, radiant with happiness. "I have seen the Lord!" she cried. But they would not share her joy – they could not believe that Jesus was alive – the news was too good to be true.

Late in the evening, into the upper room came two excited men, bringing great news.

They had been walking out to a village called Emmaus that afternoon, and talking sadly of Jesus and his death on the cross, when a stranger had joined them and walked with them. He had spoken so kindly, and comforted them so much, that they had asked him to supper with them at the inn at Emmaus.

During supper they had looked into the stranger's face, and as he broke the bread and handed it to them, the wonderful truth had come to them – it was Jesus himself! The two men had hurried straight back to Jerusalem to tell the glad news – and still the apostles found it hard to believe.

Suddenly, as they talked, someone stood in the midst of them, and said: "Peace be unto you."

It was Jesus' voice and Jesus' face.

"Why are you troubled? See my hands and feet, that it is I myself!" and Jesus showed them the wounds which the nails had made on Good Friday. Then at last the apostles knew for certain that this was indeed Jesus, their own Master, who had risen from the dead.

The news soon spread through Jerusalem and reached the chief priests that Jesus was alive again, and they questioned the soldiers who had been on guard in Joseph's garden.

The soldiers said that an angel, as bright as the lightning, had come down from heaven and rolled away the stone from the tomb, and Jesus had come forth.

Then the priests paid the soldiers large sums of money to tell everyone that the disciples had stolen Jesus' body from the tomb during the night; and many Jews believed this lie. But the priests knew that all their wicked plans had failed – Jesus had broken the power of sin and death – he had risen, glorious and triumphant.

The Ascension of Jesus

Forty days had passed since Easter Sunday, and the apostles were again in Jerusalem, walking along the well-known road towards Bethany, with Jesus.

During many walks and quiet meetings with him, they had learnt what their work was to be in future. They who had been with Jesus, listening to his teaching and seeing his wonderful works, were to tell the world all that they had heard and seen.

~

Jesus and the apostles walked on together and presently reached the top of the Mount of Olives. There Jesus gave them his last command. "Go ye, therefore, and make disciples of all nations," he said, "baptizing them in the name of the Father, and of the Son, and of the Holy Spirit. And behold I am with you always, even unto the end of the world."

Jesus then raised his hand to bless his apostles, and as he spoke, they saw a bright cloud come down from the sky, and take him from their sight.

As they stood gazing upwards they heard a voice speaking, and saw two angels, dressed in white, standing by them. "Men of Galilee," said the angels, "Why do you stand looking into Heaven? This same Jesus who has gone into Heaven, will come again, in like manner as you have seen him go."

They were not unhappy as they went down the Mount of Olives, and back to the upper room, for were not Jesus' last words ringing in their ears: "Behold, I am with you always," and they knew that this was true.

Philip the Deacon

There followed troubled times for the disciples in Jerusalem. The priests determined to prevent the spread of the Christian faith by seeking out all who were followers of Jesus and sending them to prison. But the news of Jesus' resurrection spread to nearby villages and distant towns.

Philip was walking alone down the desert road which led southwards to the country of Ethiopia. Presently he heard the sound of galloping horses; he turned and saw a chariot coming swiftly towards him. There was an Ethiopian, splendidly dressed, sitting in it, and reading from a parchment scroll.

Philip ran beside the chariot. "Do you understand what you are reading?" he cried.

The man ordered his driver to stop the horses at once. "How can I understand, unless someone shall help me?" he replied; and he begged Philip to drive with him.

Philip stepped up into the chariot, and saw that the man was reading the book of the prophet Isaiah.

Philip and the Ethiopian bent together over the writing, and read the words which foretold the coming of a great King who would suffer and die for his people.

"I pray thee, of whom speaketh the prophet?" asked the man.

Philip started from the beginning and told the wonderful story of Jesus.

Presently the road ran beside a stream of water.

"Here is water!" exclaimed the Ethiopian; "what hinders me from being baptized?"

"If you believe with all your heart, you may," replied Philip; and they went down together into the stream.

After the baptism the Ethiopian drove rapidly on his way, a happy man.

Peter in Prison

King Herod sent out soldiers to seek for the leaders of the Christian faith.

A few days before the Feast of the Passover the soldiers captured Peter; they put him into prison, where Herod meant to keep him, closely guarded, until the feast was over.

For days Peter lay in the dark prison cell, chained to two rough Roman soldiers. He was perfectly calm and happy; he knew that whatever happened would be for the best; if he were rescued it would show him that God had still some work for him to do in the world; if he were condemned to die – had not Jesus taken all fear from death?

One night, when all was quiet in the prison – the iron gates locked, the heavy outer and inner doors bolted and guarded by drowsy soldiers, and Peter's two guards sleeping heavily beside him – Peter himself was wakened by a touch on his side. He opened his eyes; his cell was full of light, and a voice said, "Rise up quickly."

Peter sat up, the chains on his wrists came unfastened and fell off, but the guards did not stir.

"Bind on your sandals," said the visitor, "put on your coat, and follow me."

Obediently Peter dressed himself, and believing that it was a dream, he followed the bright figure through the open door. They walked past the sleeping guards, across the courtyard to the iron gates. These also opened for them; the angel guide led on to the end of the street, and then disappeared.

Peter looked about him; he was alone, and free, in the well-known street.

"The Lord has sent his angel, and saved me from the

Rhoda opened the door to Peter

hand of Herod," he said to himself; and he stood still to consider where he should go. He would be sure to find some of the disciples gathered in the house of Mary, the mother of Mark. Her upper room was often used as a meeting-place; he would go there.

Peter reached the house, and knocked at the door in the courtyard wall.

He heard footsteps cross the yard, and the voice of Rhoda, the maid, asking, "Who is there?"

"It is I, Peter," he replied; and to his surprise the gate was not opened; he heard the footsteps running back to the house.

Peter heard many people crossing the courtyard, and voices saying, "You must be mad! It cannot be Peter – it is his angel!" Then the gate was unbolted and flung open.

By the light of a little lamp which Rhoda held up, Peter could see the astonished faces of his friends peering out at him. He told them the wonderful story of his deliverance from prison, and they praised God for this answer to the prayers which they had prayed night and day for Peter.

A search would be made for Peter, but no one had seen him leave his cell, so Herod would never know how his prisoner had escaped.

The Conversion of Saul

Many did not believe that Jesus of Nazareth was the promised Messiah.

Saul of Tarsus did not believe; he helped the priests in their cruel persecution of the followers of Jesus. How little they knew that this persecution was a means of spreading the faith still farther.

When he heard that the Christian faith was spreading beyond Jerusalem, Saul set off for Damascus, to seek out and imprison the disciples there.

Suddenly a great light from heaven shone round him, and, for a moment, Saul saw a figure standing in the light; then he hid his face and fell to the ground.

"Saul, Saul!" said a voice, "why do you persecute me?"

"Who are you, Lord?" asked Saul, but he already knew the answer.

"I am Jesus," replied the voice.

"What shall I do, Lord?" asked Saul at last.

"Arise, and go into Damascus," came the answer, "and you shall be told what to do."

Slowly Saul rose to his feet; he opened his eyes, but he could not see – the brilliant light had blinded him. He held out his hands to his companions, who led him to the city.

For three days Saul would neither eat nor drink, he wished only to think and pray, for all his life was changed now. He had seen Jesus – he believed in Jesus – and he knew that in hurting Jesus' followers he had hurt himself.

On the third day a disciple came to the house. Saul felt a kind hand laid on his shoulder, and heard a friendly voice saying, "Brother Saul, the Lord Jesus has sent me, that you may receive your sight."

On the road to Damascus

Saul opened his eyes, and to his joy he could see again! He was baptised that very day, and went to join the disciples, who gave him a brotherly welcome.

Saul of Tarsus, who was called by his Roman name of Paul after his baptism, worked as hard for the Church as he had once worked against it. He and the other disciples preached the good news far and wide, until large numbers joined the Christian church and they too spread the message of Jesus.

~

Thousands of years have passed since the beginning, when God made the heavens and the earth. The story which began then is still not ended, but it will end when the same Jesus who lived, loved, died, and rose again for us, comes again, and lives with us forever.

HYMNS

Jesus Shall Reign

Jesus Shall Reign

Jesus shall reign where'er the sun
Does his successive journeys run;
His kingdoms stretch from shore to shore,
Till moons shall wax and wane no more.

People and realms of every tongue
Dwell on his love with sweetest song,
And infant voices shall proclaim
Their early blessings on his name.

Blessings abound where'er he reigns;
The prisoner leaps to lose his chains;
The weary find eternal rest,
And all the sons of want are blest.

Let every creature rise and bring
Peculiar honours to our King;
Angels descend with songs again,
And earth repeat the long amen.

We Plough the Fields

We plough the fields and scatter
The good seed on the land,
But it is fed and watered
By God's almighty hand;
He sends the snow in winter,
The warmth to swell the grain,
The breezes and the sunshine,
And soft refreshing rain.
All good gifts around us
Are sent from Heav'n above,
Then thank the Lord,
O thank the Lord,
For all His love.

He only is the Maker
Of all things near and far;
He paints the wayside flower;
He lights the evening star;
The winds and waves obey Him;
By Him the birds are fed;
Much more to us, His children,
He gives our daily bread.
All good gifts around us
Are sent from Heav'n above,
Then thank the Lord,
O thank the Lord,
For all His love.

We Plough the Fields

The King of Love

The King of Love

The King of Love my Shepherd is,
  Whose goodness faileth never;
  I nothing lack if I am His
  And He is mine forever.

Where streams of living water flow
  My ransomed soul He leadeth,
And, where the verdant pastures grow,
  With food celestial feedeth.

Perverse and foolish oft I strayed,
  But yet in love He sought me,
And on His shoulder gently laid,
  And home, rejoicing, brought me.

In death's dark vale I fear no ill
  With Thee, dear Lord, beside me;
Thy rod and staff my comfort still,
  Thy Cross before to guide me.

Thou spread'st a table in my sight;
  Thy unction grace bestoweth:
And oh, what transport of delight
  From Thy pure chalice floweth!

And so through all the length of days
  Thy goodness faileth never:
Good Shepherd, may I sing Thy praise
  Within Thy house for ever.

♦ 79 ♦

Onward, Christian Soldiers

Onward, Christian soldiers,
Marching as to war,
With the cross of Jesus
Going on before.
Christ, the Royal Master,
Leads against the foe;
Forward into battle,
See, His banners go!
Onward, Christian soldiers,
Marching as to war,
With the cross of Jesus
Going on before.

At the sign of triumph
Satan's host doth flee;
On then, Christian soldiers,
On to victory!
Hell's foundations quiver
At the shout of praise;
Brothers, lift your voices,
Loud your anthems raise.
Onward, Christian soldiers,
Marching as to war,
With the cross of Jesus
Going on before.

Like a mighty army
Moves the Church of God;
Brothers, we are treading
Where the saints have trod;
We are not divided,
All one body we,
One in hope and doctrine,
One in charity.
Onward, Christian soldiers,
Marching as to war,
With the cross of Jesus
Going on before.

Onward, Christian Soldiers

All Things Bright and Beautiful

All Things Bright and Beautiful

All things bright and beautiful,
All creatures great and small,
All things wise and wonderful,
The Lord God made them all.

Each little flow'r that opens,
Each little bird that sings,
He made their glowing colours,
He made their tiny wings.

All things bright and beautiful,
All creatures great and small,
All things wise and wonderful,
The Lord God made them all.

The purple-headed mountain,
The river running by,
The sunset, and the morning
That brightens up the sky;

All things bright and beautiful,
All creatures great and small,
All things wise and wonderful,
The Lord God made them all.

The cold wind in the winter,
The pleasant summer sun,
The ripe fruits in the garden,
He made them every one;

All things bright and beautiful,
All creatures great and small,
All things wise and wonderful,
The Lord God made them all.

The tall trees in the greenwood,
The meadows where we play,
The rushes by the water,
We gather every day;

All things bright and beautiful,
All creatures great and small,
All things wise and wonderful,
The Lord God made them all.

He gave us eyes to see them,
And lips that we might tell,
How great is God Almighty,
Who has made all things well.

All things bright and beautiful,
All creatures great and small,
All things wise and wonderful,
The Lord God made them all.

Love Divine

Love divine, all loves excelling,
Joy of heaven to earth come down,
Fix in us Thy humble dwelling,
All Thy faithful mercies crown.

Jesus, Thou art all compassion,
Pure, unbounded love Thou art;
Visit us with Thy salvation,
Enter ev'ry trembling heart.

Come, Almighty, to deliver,
Let us all Thy life receive;
Come to us, dear Lord, and never,
Never more Thy temples leave.

Thee we would be always blessing;
Serve Thee as Thy hosts above;
Pray, and praise Thee without ceasing;
Glory in Thy perfect love.

Love Divine

Children of the Heavenly King

Children of the Heavenly King

Children of the Heavenly King,
As ye journey sweetly sing;
Sing your Saviour's worthy praise,
Glorious in his works and ways.

We are travelling home to God,
In the way the fathers trod;
They are happy now, and we
Soon their happiness shall see.

Fear not, brethren; joyful stand
On the borders of your land:
Jesus Christ, your Father's Son,
Bids you undismayed go on.

Lord, obediently we go,
Gladly leaving all below:
Only thou our Leader be
And we still will follow thee.

The Shepherd Boy's Song

The Shepherd Boy's Song

He that is down needs fear no fall,
He that is low, no pride;
He that is humble ever shall
Have God to be his guide.

I am content with what I have,
Little be it or much:
And, Lord, contentment still I crave,
Because thou savest such.

Fullness to such a burden is
That goes on pilgrimage:
Here little, and hereafter bliss,
Is best from age to age.

Dear Lord and Father of Mankind

Dear Lord and Father of mankind,
Forgive our foolish ways!
Re-clothe us in our rightful mind,
In purer lives Thy service find,
In deeper reverence praise.
In deeper reverence praise.

In simple trust like theirs who heard,
Beside the Syrian sea,
The gracious calling of the Lord,
Let us, like them, without a word
Rise up and follow Thee.
Rise up and follow Thee.

O Sabbath rest by Galilee!
O calm of hills above,
Where Jesus knelt to share with Thee
The silence of eternity,
Interpreted by love!
Interpreted by love!

Drop Thy still dews of quietness,
Till all our strivings cease;
Take from our souls the strain and stress,
And let our ordered lives confess
The beauty of Thy peace.
The beauty of Thy peace.

Dear Lord and Father of Mankind

Breathe through the heats of our desire
Thy coolness and Thy balm;
Let sense be dumb, let flesh retire;
Speak through the earthquake, wind, and fire,
O still small voice of calm!
O still small voice of calm!

Praise to the Lord,
the Almighty

Praise to the Lord, the Almighty, the King of creation!
O my soul, praise Him, for He is your health and salvation.
All you who hear, now to His altar draw near,
Join in profound adoration.

Praise to the Lord, let us offer our gifts at His altar;
Let not our sins and transgressions now cause us to falter.
Christ, the High Priest, bids us all join in His feast,
Victims with Him on the altar.

Praise to the Lord, oh, let all that is in us adore Him!
All that has life and breath, come now in praises before Him.
Let the Amen sound from His people again,
Now as we worship before Him.

All Glory, Laud and Honour

All glory, laud, and honour
To Thee, Redeemer, King,
To Whom the lips of children
Made sweet Hosannas ring!
Thou art the King of Israel,
Thou David's Royal Son,
Who in the Lord's name comest,
The King and Blessèd One.

All glory, laud, and honour
To Thee, Redeemer, King,
To Whom the lips of children
Made sweet Hosannas ring!
The company of angels
Are praising Thee on high,
And mortal men, and all things
Created make reply.

All glory, laud, and honour
To Thee, Redeemer, King,
To Whom the lips of children
Made sweet Hosannas ring!
The people of the Hebrews
With palms before Thee went,
Our praise and prayer and anthems
Before Thee we present.

All glory, laud, and honour
To Thee, Redeemer, King,
To Whom the lips of children
Made sweet Hosannas ring!
To Thee before Thy Passion
They sang their hymns of praise,
To Thee now high exalted,
Our melody we raise.

All Glory, Laud and Honour

A Great and Mighty Wonder

A Great and Mighty Wonder

A great and mighty wonder,
A full and holy cure!
The Virgin bears the Infant
With virgin-honour pure.
Repeat the hymn again!
"To God on high be glory,
And peace on earth to men!"

The Word becomes incarnate
And yet remains on high!
And Cherubim sing anthems
To shepherds from the sky.
Repeat the hymn again!
"To God on high be glory,
And peace on earth to men!"

While thus they sing your Monarch,
Those bright angelic bands,
Rejoice, ye vales and mountains,
Ye oceans clap your hands.
Repeat the hymn again!
"To God on high be glory,
And peace on earth to men!"

Since all He comes to ransom,
By all be He adored,
The Infant born in Bethl'em,
The Saviour and the Lord.
Repeat the hymn again!
"To God on high be glory,
And peace on earth to men!"

On Christmas Day
in the Morning

(From the Carol "I Saw Three Ships")

And all the bells on earth shall ring,
On Christmas Day, on Christmas Day,
And all the bells on earth shall ring
On Christmas Day in the morning.

And all the Angels in heaven shall sing,
On Christmas Day, on Christmas Day,
And all the Angels in heaven shall sing
On Christmas Day in the morning.

And all the souls on earth shall sing,
On Christmas Day, on Christmas Day,
And all the souls on earth shall sing
On Christmas Day in the morning.

Then let us all rejoice amain,
On Christmas Day, on Christmas Day,
Then let us all rejoice amain
On Christmas Day in the morning.

Christmas Carol

The snow lay on the ground,
the star shone bright,
When Christ our Lord was born
on Christmas night,
When Christ our Lord was born
on Christmas night.

'Twas Mary, daughter pure of Holy Ann,
That brought Him to this world,
our Lord made man,
That brought Him to this world,
our Lord made man.

She laid Him on the straw at Bethlehem,
The ass and oxen shared the roof
with them,
The ass and oxen shared the roof
with them.

O Come, All Ye Faithful

O come, all ye faithful,
Joyful and triumphant;
O come ye, O come ye
    to Bethlehem;
Come and behold Him
Born the King of Angels;
O come, let us adore Him,
O come, let us adore Him,
O come, let us adore Him,
    Christ the Lord.

God of God,
    Light of Light,
Lo! He abhors not the Virgin's womb;
    Very God,
    Begotten, not created;
O come, let us adore Him,
O come, let us adore Him,
O come, let us adore Him,
    Christ the Lord.

Sing, choirs of angels,
    Sing in exultation,
Sing, all ye citizens of
    heaven above,
    Glory to God
    In the highest;
O come, let us adore Him,
O come, let us adore Him,
O come, let us adore Him,
    Christ the Lord.

Yea, Lord, we greet Thee,
Born this happy morning;
Jesu, to Thee be glory given;
Word of the Father,
Now in flesh appearing;
O come, let us adore Him,
O come, let us adore Him,
O come, let us adore Him,
    Christ the Lord.

O Come, All Ye Faithful

Christ the Lord is Risen Again

Christ the Lord is risen again; *Alleluya!*
Christ hath broken every chain; *Alleluya!*
Hark, angelic voices cry, *Alleluya!*
Singing evermore on high *Alleluya!*

He Who bore all pain and loss, *Alleluya!*
Comfortless upon the Cross, *Alleluya!*
Lives in glory now on high, *Alleluya!*
Pleads for us and hears our cry; *Alleluya!*

Thou, our Paschal Lamb indeed, *Alleluya!*
Christ, Thy ransomed people feed: *Alleluya!*
Take our sins and guilt away, *Alleluya!*
Let us sing by night and day, *Alleluya!*

Away in a Manger

Away in a manger, no crib for a bed,
The little Lord Jesus lay down His sweet head,
The stars in the bright sky looked down where He lay,
The little Lord Jesus asleep on the hay.

The cattle are lowing, the Baby awakes,
But little Lord Jesus no crying He makes.
I love Thee, Lord Jesus! look down from the sky,
And stay by my side until morning is nigh.

Be near me, Lord Jesus; I ask Thee to stay
Close by me for ever, and love me, I pray.
Bless all the dear children in Thy tender care,
And fit us for heaven, to live with Thee there.

While Shepherds Watched

While Shepherds Watched

While shepherds watched their flocks by night,
All seated on the ground,
The angel of the Lord came down,
And glory shone around.

"Fear not," said he; for mighty dread
Had seized their troubled mind;
"Glad tidings of great joy I bring
To you and all mankind.

"To you in David's town this day
Is born of David's line
A Saviour, Who is Christ the Lord:
And this shall be the sign:

"The heavenly Babe you there shall find
To human view displayed,
All meanly wrapped in swathing bands,
And in a manger laid."

Thus spake the seraph; and forthwith
Appeared a shining throng
Of angels praising God, who thus
Addressed their joyful song:

"All glory be to God on high,
And in the earth be peace;
Goodwill henceforth from Heaven to men
Begin and never cease."

Once in Royal David's City

Once in royal David's city
Stood a lowly cattle shed,
Where a mother laid her Baby
In a manger for His bed:
Mary was that mother mild,
Jesus Christ her little Child.

He came down to earth from heaven
Who is God and Lord of all,
And His shelter was a stable,
And His cradle was a stall;
With the poor, and mean, and lowly,
Lived on earth our Saviour holy.

And through all His wondrous childhood,
He would honour and obey,
Love, and watch the lowly maiden
In whose gentle arms He lay;
Christian children all must be
Mild, obedient, good as He.

For He is our childhood's pattern;
Day be day like us He grew;
He was little, weak and helpless,
Tears and smiles like us He knew;
And He feeleth for our sadness,
And He shareth in our gladness.

Once in Royal David's City

PRAYERS

God be thanked

A Traditional Grace

What God gives, and what we take,
'Tis a gift for Christ His sake:
Be the meal of Beans and Pease
God be thanked for those, and these:
Have we flesh, or have we fish,
All are Fragments from His dish.

Grace Before Meat
Three Very Old Graces

I
Bless these Thy gifts, most gracious God,
From whom all goodness springs;
Make clean our hearts and feed our souls
With good and joyful things.

II
Pray we to God, the Almighty Lord,
That sendeth food to beasts and men,
To send His blessing on this board,
To feed us now and ever. Amen.

III
God bless our meat,
God guide our ways,
God give us grace
Our Lord to please.
Lord, long preserve in peace and health
Our gracious Queen Elizabeth.

Grace Before Meat

Littles
(From "A Ternarie of Littles")

A little Saint best fits
a little Shrine,
As little Prop best fits
a little Vine,
As my small Cruse best
fits my little Wine.

A little Seed best fits a little Soil,
A little Trade best fits a little Toil,
As my small Jar best fits my little Oil.

A little Bin best fits a little Bread,
A little Garland fits a little Head,
As my small Stuff best fits my little Shed.

A little Hearth best
fits a little Fire,
A little Chapel best
fits a little Choir,
As my small Bell best
fits my little Spire.

A little Stream best fits a little Boat,
A little Lead best fits a little Float,
As my small Pipe best fits my little Note.

The Lord's My Shepherd

The Lord's My Shepherd

The Lord's my shepherd, I'll not want.
He makes me down to lie
In pastures green; He leadeth me
The quiet waters by.

My soul He doth restore again;
And me to walk doth make
Within the paths of righteousness,
E'en for His own name's sake.

Yea, though I walk in death's dark vale,
Yet will I fear none ill;
For Thou art with me, and Thy rod
And staff me comfort still.

My table Thou hast furnished
In presence of my foes;
My head thou dost with oil anoint,
And my cup overflows.

The Lamb

Little Lamb, who made thee?
Dost thou know who made thee,
Gave thee life, and bade thee feed
By the stream and o'er the mead;
　Gave thee clothing of delight,
　Softest clothing, woolly, bright;
　Gave thee such a tender voice,
　Making all the vales rejoice?
Little Lamb, who made thee?
Dost thou know who made thee?

Little Lamb, I'll tell thee,
　Little Lamb, I'll tell thee;
　He is callèd by thy name,
For He calls Himself a Lamb.
He is meek, and He is mild,
　He became a little child.
I a child, and thou a lamb,
We are callèd by His name.
　Little Lamb, God Bless thee!
　Little Lamb, God Bless thee!

He Prayeth Well

He prayeth well, who loveth well
Both man and bird and beast.
He prayeth best, who loveth best
All things both great and small;
For the dear God who loveth us,
He made and loveth all.

Prayer at Bedtime

Matthew, Mark, Luke, and John,
Bless the bed that I lie on.
Four corners to my bed,
Four Angels there be spread:
One at the head, one at the feet,
And two to guard me while I sleep.
God within, and God without,
And Jesus Christ all round about;
If any danger come to me,
Sweet Jesus Christ deliver me.
Before I lay me down to sleep
I give my soul to Christ to keep;
And if I die before I wake,
I pray that Christ my soul will take.

Prayer at Bedtime